# The Act of Dying

*by*

# Lucretia Voigt

*Finishing Line Press*
Georgetown, Kentucky

# The Act of Dying

*For the ones who have passed through my life and left their mark, an invisible scar that makes itself known like a pebble caught in my shoe. May the pain from your passing never leave me. It helps me remember.*

Copyright © 2025 by Lucretia Voigt
ISBN 979-8-89990-088-4 First Edition
All rights reserved under International and Pan-American Copyright Conventions. No part of this book may be reproduced in any manner whatsoever without written permission from the publisher, except in the case of brief quotations embodied in critical articles and reviews.

Publisher: Leah Huete de Maines
Editor: Christen Kincaid
Cover Art: Lucretia Voigt
Author Photo: Lucretia Voigt
Cover Design: Elizabeth Maines McCleavy

Order online: www.finishinglinepress.com
also available on amazon.com

Author inquiries and mail orders:
Finishing Line Press
PO Box 1626
Georgetown, Kentucky 40324
USA

# Contents

Stuck ........................................................................................... 1

## Act I

We are birthed in music .......................................................... 5
Strands ..................................................................................... 6
Planting Season ....................................................................... 7
The Act of Dying .................................................................... 8
Dusk ......................................................................................... 9
On Saturday nights he washed our hair .............................. 10
Beauty .................................................................................... 11
Darkness ................................................................................ 12
Unrequited Trust .................................................................. 13
Forgiven ................................................................................. 15
Lost in Translation ............................................................... 16
Moon Boots ........................................................................... 17
The Act of Dying .................................................................. 18
Quilting .................................................................................. 19
I put your boots on today .................................................... 20
New Moon ............................................................................. 21
Watching a Documentary on "The History of Ancient Britain" ................ 22
Another Anniversary ............................................................ 23

## Act II

Depression Comes Calling ................................................... 27
Same time every day ............................................................ 28
56 Times ................................................................................ 29
Survival .................................................................................. 30

The Act of Dying ........................................................................... 31
Blue ................................................................................................ 32
Marigold ........................................................................................ 33
Keeping Watch .............................................................................. 34

## Act III

Knowing ........................................................................................ 39
Deluge ............................................................................................ 40
I ate the mango ............................................................................. 42
Life ................................................................................................. 43
There are days I think you are a bird ......................................... 44
Break .............................................................................................. 46
Hummingbird Season .................................................................. 47
A Year of Firsts ............................................................................. 48
Counting Minutes ........................................................................ 49
Wildfire .......................................................................................... 50
Ice Storm ....................................................................................... 51
When Spring Is a Lie You Tell Yourself ..................................... 52
Temporary Permanence .............................................................. 53
Hope ............................................................................................... 54
Redemption ................................................................................... 55

Acknowledgments ........................................................................ 56

*The act of dying is one of the acts of life.*

—Marcus Aurelius

**Stuck**

Between the first idea and the second
is a chasm, a trench dug down
in loam, interrupted roots of
trees and plants poke
through the sides. Caught
in mid-sentence they hang
in question marks and
hyphens. I find myself
spending too much time
down here, watching clouds
flit by as spindly limbs sway
overhead, listening to the chitterings

of squirrels. A birch tree stands guard
at the entrance, its trunk forks
once, then twice, yet again,
a good climbing tree if
I were younger and dreaming
those dreams of reaching
the sky.

I watch as the birch tree sheds a layer of bark.
No, it's a sparrow.
No, it's the wind.

# Act I

**We are birthed in music**

> Our mamas and aunts whisper weathered quilt lullabies as they rock us to sleep. Heady honeysuckle breezes tousle our hair. In the staccato calls of cardinals, the trills of Kentucky warblers, the shrill half-notes of chickadees, we hear songs before we learn to talk. We are told stories of coal mines and collapses, of thistled dirt roads and hard-scrabble farming. We are taught to pray—for forgiveness, for gratitude, for existence. Creek water is a passage to redemption. We dream of promised mockingbirds if we hush and don't say a word. We learn early to be cautious of boughs breaking. We hold our breath when hearses go by to keep ourselves from laughing, listen for salvation in bluegrass notes
>
>> that wrap around us
>> like brackish muck
>> in a coal slurry pond.

**Strands**

Every night after *Wheel of Fortune* but before
the 10 o'clock news I'd take down
her hairbrush from atop the cherry
dresser she received as a wedding gift
and carried from Martha, Kentucky to Ashland
over 60 years back. During the day

she kept her hair in a bun, black pins
holding the neat spiral atop her head.
Barely 5'3" in her Sunday shoes,
she let her hair grow long, long
enough to stand on. We would sit
in cane chairs on the screened-in
sunporch, listen to the mating calls
of cicadas, watch for fireflies.

While I brushed, she would talk, tell stories
of her life, how she ferried a flat raft across
Blaine Creek as an 8-year old, how God
spoke to her as she walked on the old wagon road
that ran along Lower Laurel Creek. She told me
how my great-grandfather Gusty designed and built
their home, laying oak floorboards as she watched,
the same floorboards below our bare feet.

I would take my time, work my way
down, until I was sitting on the
floor, holding in my hands these strands
of silver that were older than me, releasing
them as the wispy ends
twisted in the summer breeze
back upon themselves.

**Planting Season**

His hands, the color
of the dirt he mounds around
sweet potato plants

tender green tendrils
poke out as yellow flowers
reach upward for sun

*This is the fun part,*
he smiles, water I poured trans-
forming dust to mud

I can imagine
him as a young boy making
mud pies, hands dirty

when my grandmother
calls him for dinner on late
hazy summer nights

Now eighty-two, he
has his own children, grandchild-
ren, great-grandchildren

Twirling the spade in
darkness, he readies earth for
the next plant, again

He kneels on the tilled
ground, moves down the row slowly
in a kind of prayer

**The Act of Dying**

There is a nanosecond, a twitch so fast and minute that we don't even feel it, where we cross from living　　　　to dead,　　　　from　　　present tense　　　　　　　　to past. A pin prick of time. A moment so quick we are unaware it has happened.　　　　Scientists in Canada recently proved that thirty seconds before and after our heart quits pumping blood, our brainwaves follow the same patterns as when we dream. For thirty seconds, our brains refuse to believe it is the end. Sometimes we spend time in the act of dying, holding on　　　　　　　　　　　　as　　our heart struggles to pump blood to our brain.　　　The longest someone has stayed in a coma, holding on to the ledge,　　　　refusing to give up, is 37 years and 111 days.　　　Elaine Esposito was 6 years old when she went to the hospital for a routine appendectomy.
　　　She never left.

# Dusk

"I need to go help daddy in the garden,"
her voice a warble, unfocused
eyes wide, as she brings the china
saucer brimming with tea to her lips,
just like her momma taught her.

> *That ain't your daddy. Gusty passed on over*
> *five years ago. That's David, your son.*

"He'll be mad if I don't help," her
voice soft, as out the window
the landscape wavers, she sees the well
she'll need to pump later to bring water
in to wash the dishes and clothes.

> *Finish up your tea, now, so I can get on*
> *with my chores. Then we'll go sit a spell*
> *on the porch.*

"I'll just sneak off the porch and help him, I will,"
a smile plays on her lips, each sip of tea
a gathered memory. Through the window
she smells the readied soil, blue runners ripe
for picking, Kentucky Stripe tomatoes laden
with juice, dipping to kiss the ground.

**On Saturday nights he washed our hair**

as we played in the white porcelain
tub, swirling pictures on the tile wall with Ivory
soap, castles with pointed turrets, a moat to keep the dragons out.

We shaped white beehives, tri-cornered hats, Pippi Long-
stocking pigtails, with *Johnson's No More Tears*
shampoo, then a baptismal dunk and final rinse.

My sister, who could reach the top dresser
drawer, helped me into my Snow White
nightgown, while she wore Cinderella.

We lay on the fold out couch, our wet hair
leaving imprints on the white cotton
pillows, my single father in the middle, his arms encircling us.

**Beauty**

Her hair black as the coal
her daddy shoveled into
the coke furnace at Armco
Steel, eyes green as the unopened
gardenia bud, bright as a full moon
on a clear winter night.

She traded on her looks, hid
her mind under crimson lipstick
and frosted pink blush, used Cosmopolitan
and Glamour as templates until the edges
became dull and ragged,
subject to a steady stream
of alcohol and tears.

In the one picture I have
she is staring at the camera,
hair in a *That Girl!* flip, sitting
at a table strewn with empty
glasses, hands clasped
in her lap.

I cut her last husband
out of that photo, staring
at her and not the camera,
the husband who tiptoed
into my room with bloodshot
bourbon eyes, whispered
how I was lucky
that I looked just like her.

**Darkness**

in this holler, wet with morning dew, the mountains

                                                                hem me in

                fog hangs low, spider

        web of condensation strung
                    between these peaks of poplars and oaks

     like those threadbare sheets and
     blankets held aloft by chairs and tables
     where I would hide, flashlight
     and book in hand, pretending
     to be anywhere but here

**Unrequited Trust**

They hobbled her
        because she needed to be
                              still—
this horse who was injured but worth saving.

Curiosity in her eyes
        of their movement and
                the new hardware quickly
                              moved to fear,
pupils dilated into

        shrouded pools, high-pitched
                              whinnies, unsure.

The first day was the worst—lashing out, trying to
                              move, fighting against the
    tethers, whipping her head
        from side to side.

                Eventually she quieted.

Flaring nostrils
        became the only evidence
                of the agitation
                      below the surface.

For a time she refused to eat,

                grasping control
                              in the only way left.

From that point on,
        even after the shackles
                were removed, the injury
                        healed, her eyes were always
                                        questioning,

as if in trying to save
her they had betrayed
her, taking her freedom
as easily as grabbing
the reins.

**Forgiven**

We memorized Bible verses like
our friends did batting averages
or the words to Cheap Trick's
*I Want You To Want Me.*

Our parents made sure
if the church doors were open
we were there—
Sunday morning
Sunday School
Sunday night worship
Wednesday night fellowship.

Church camp
Revivals
Altar calls to Amazing Grace—
we would cheat—peek
through barely open eyes
to see who among us
had sins to confess.

When my brother told me
over dumplings at China Wok—
my first trip home from
Trevecca Nazarene College—
that after graduation
he would never go back—
*Church and I don't mix—*
I understood.

We measured love against
the wrath of God, scared
of the communion wafer
that could damn our unrepentant
souls to hell, scared
of the empty house, sure
the rapture had come and
left us behind.

**Lost in Translation**

He said the doctor said
a virus caused his heart to race.

Does the Oxycontin work like a Rosetta Stone translating

        *acute arrhythmia due to intravenous oxycontin abuse*
to
        *flu?*

How deep does the rewiring go?

When I tell him, "I love you
and I'm worried," do the words
enter his ear like mosquitoes
at nightfall, annoy as only a sister can?

That last trip home, we harmonized
bluegrass songs, our breath caught
in memories of soccer matches and
Chinese food, harvesting half-runners
and frying okra. Did my words get lost
among the Bible verses we memorized
as children, like the cardinal's song
on a foggy morning?

What did he hear instead?

**Moon Boots**

You pushed me up
and down our long hallway, running
behind the spaceship we decorated
together, a box rescued
from the garbage, the friction
with the carpet heating
the cardboard beneath me.

Sometimes you would turn the hall light off and I could believe that I was
hurtling through space instead of Ferguson Drive in Ashland, Kentucky.

So today when I saw the Moon Boots at
Ocean State Job Lot, while you waited
in the car for me to buy shower
shoes, a bathrobe, a toothbrush—I couldn't
help myself. I know I don't need
Moon Boots in rehab. But I thought maybe
they would make you smile.

I slipped my feet into those mesmerizing
silver blocks, felt the bounce of that first
small step, cut the tag off with the Swiss
army knife I keep on my keychain, and
walked out the automatic doors.

### The Act of Dying

My brother's banjo was placed in his casket with him, his hand rested on the dark stain on the banjo head, evidence of years spent picking *Foggy Mountain Breakdown* and *I'll Fly Away*, his fingers an extension of his soul, the maple neck laid across his body as if he could pick it up and play.        Brent loved that banjo.  It was the one thing he pawned for drug money that he would always go back and get.    But like the sun that creeps up over the Kentucky mountains, blinding as it crests, drug overdose deaths have risen. Between 1999 and 2019 deaths due to heroin rose from        0.07 percent per 100,000         to 4.9 percent.   In 2008, drug overdoses killed 36,500.
            That year the population of my hometown
                            of Ashland, Kentucky was 21,332.

## Quilting

I cut rectangles and squares
from the shirts he left
behind, the cotton oxfords
worn when playing
with that gospel group, the name
which escapes me now and no one
seems to remember. I should have sold
his Phish t-shirts on eBay, but instead
have traced patterns around the logos, ovals
and stars to applique, reconstructing
the pieces, rainbow colors
and words against the staid
blue and white cotton. I keep adding
rows, rectangles from the linen dress shirt
worn to our sister Bri's wedding, the one
he's wearing in the last picture
where our family is all together.
Arms rest across each other's
shoulders, a crazy quilt line
of heights and smiles, burgundies
and pastels, joined together
by an invisible whipstitch
of longing.

**I put your boots on today**

the ones you wore hiking
Roan Mountain the Spring
Break you walked that portion
of the Appalachian Trail with Dad.

The lace on the right boot is broken—
I tied the ends together with a double
fisherman's knot, the one knot, you said,
every person should know. The watermark

still shows above the left heel,
probably from your wading in
too far when helping a kayaker stranded
on a shoal. A friend said I could buff it out,

take saddle soap,
work the stain in
until it disappears.
But I'd rather wade in further,

watch as the clear water
glides past the stain,
up the knotted lace,
feel its brisk caress
as it weighs me down.

*for Brent (8/10/72—11/23/08)*

**New Moon**

In these mountains, darkness is a hand-sewn funeral dress.
Moth-eaten holes let the stars shine through.

The new moon indigo turns
the dirt path between our houses
treacherous, gives cover to the coyote
that's been pilfering the chickens.

My people planted by the signs,
canned our vegetables by the phases
of the moon. I sit on the porch,

hear the rustle of dancing sprites
in the leaves of the poplars, wait
for my eyes to adjust.

It is not the darkness I mind
but the emptiness—
the missing boots by the door, muddy
from hiking the ridge, the silent banjo
locked in its case, growing dusty
in the corner, the cast iron cornbread pan,
cold and empty in the cupboard.

### Watching a documentary on "The History of Ancient Britain"

I want to be cremated when I die.
I don't want some archeologist
or treasure hunter digging
with visions of gold
tens of thousands of years
from now to come across
my skeleton, an assemblage
of bones and teeth that have
refused to disintegrate.

I don't want my bones
pieced back together
like a second-hand
jigsaw puzzle, strangers
concocting stories about
the healed ulna, the deviated
septum, hypothesizing the
damage to the bones was
caused by nature or wild
animals, making them the villians
instead of an alcoholic
boyfriend who finished
arguments with
exclamation points
of twisted arms. I want

my story to have an ending,
one where there is no possibility
of a sequel written by someone
who only reads the Cliffs notes, to have
those chapters burned like a solstice
ritual, and erase proof of the pain,
the calcified shame
cleansed by fire.

**Another Anniversary**

Each year the date creeps
up on me like kudzu
on a Southern White Oak

another year since my brother
left on heroin-laced
fog, needle sticking
in his arm when the
paramedics found him.

Hindus make
offerings to their
loved one on the
anniversary of their
passing, elaborate
meals, incense and
gifts put on an altar
in remembrance

Catholics pray, light
candles, ask for the lost
souls to be ushered
from purgatory
straight to heaven

I take off my boots,
walk into the woods.

# Act II

**Depression Comes Calling**

This morning the frost
trapped the fallow
ground, and a halo nestled
around the noonday sun—

It is time

    to shutter the drapes, measure
        perfect cups of flour, and

bake bread.

There is a therapy to kneading
    the dough, watching it rise, twisting
        and forming each loaf,
  so I keep the oven
warm, bake one after
    another: whole wheat and
        rye, cinnamon and struan.

When I finally hear the knock
at my door, this time I'll be ready

    to invite him in, brush the
      dust from his weathered
        coat, fold him in a reluctant

embrace. I'll take down
my Mother's porcelain teacups,
pour a bourbon neat
and break bread together.

**Same time every day**

We shuffle to the hall outside the nurse's station, our rubber-soled slippers gripping linoleum flooring, and jostle for the three lone chairs, neon green against the scuffed white wall. Others are content to stand. Art therapy is over and dinnertime hasn't come. We've sung show tunes in the common room to a tone deaf piano, worked puzzles with missing pieces, now wait for our names to be called. For an acknowledgment that *yes*, you are here at McLean Mental Hospital, and *yes*, you must be medicated to survive this world, and *yes*, suicide is not the answer, and *yes*, it is not your time to go, and *yes*, if you take your medicine and participate in group therapy you might get privileges, and *yes*, we do know what's good for you, and *yes*, the windows are barred and you can only dream how the snow outside would feel on your bare feet, and *no*, you don't have a choice, and *yes*, the doors are locked and cannot be opened by you.

**56 Times**

It takes ten years for crimson red trumpet vine flowers to appear. Shame
is a red plum

left too long on the tree. The sins of the mother curl like tendrils
around the children.

The sins of the mother are both sins of omission and commission. The word
*sin* is used

four hundred forty-eight times in the Bible. Forgiveness is found only
fifty-six times.

Forgiveness is found in a mountain stream hushed with fall leaves.
Even immersion can't

cleanse my soul. A juniper tree will thrive on rocks, its roots finding
cracks to survive.

The juniper tree is one of the slowest growing plants. Let me sleep
under your branches, wake to birdsongs that sound like hope instead of guilt.

Guilt is a substitute for penance. The average person
keeps thirteen secrets, five of which they never tell.

Let me hold your secrets in my scarred hands, feel darkness glide
through my fingers. Let me cry you a river of redemption.

Redemption is a hummingbird in a sky filled with hawks.
Blood is the color of both guilt and forgiveness.

**Survival**

Morning air
thick with saltwater

We go down to the Creeks
at low tide, empty
sailboats clanging
a percussive song.
Terns and plovers skitter
looking for
breakfast. The snowy
egret peers out from the
marsh, stands apart, watching.

Pi runs after them, attempting
to herd. It is his nature.
Met with a lack of sheep
he tries to make do
with birds. They take to the air and
thinking he can join them
                                  he jumps -

I leave the oyster and scallop shells
behind, search instead for rocks,
hunt for an unbroken ring, the sign
of a wishing stone. Met with a lack of
mountains, the sassafras scent
of birch trees, the weathered wrinkles
of tulip poplar trees, I try and make do
                                  with the sea.

## The Act of Dying

When I found my husband Mark on the kitchen floor,     my brain couldn't tell me he was dead.     I kept asking him what had happened, expecting an answer.               Shock after a death is immediate and lasts for a few days to several weeks, can result in inappropriate reactions, such as laughing hysterically, can remove all memory of the first moments and days after the trauma of finding a loved one dead.
Mark's last nanosecond had dropped hours before,     but it didn't end until I saw him. In 2021, the life expectancy for a Massachusetts male was 77.9 years of age. If they retired at 65 they would have 13 years to move to Florida to escape the cold, learn to scuba dive, buy a Harley, travel to the Grand Canyon, take up bridge.                    Mark was 58.
After shock wears off,                  the grieving process begins. Uncontrollable crying at inopportune times, such as grocery shopping or waiting in line for prescription refills, is normal.
                    Everything has changed. Nothing is normal.

iii. The first glacier was formed around 34 million years ago. Humans have only been walking the planet for 6 million years. Last year the earth lost 1.2 trillion tons of ice.

**Blue**

Holbrook's eyes are ice blue, the color deep inside glaciers.[i] There has always been an innocence to his eyes. When he was born, a parade of nurses visited our room, hoping to catch him awake. His eyes make you smile. It's not magic - but it feels like it - that a brown-eyed boy named Mark and a green-eyed girl named Lucretia could together create a blue-eyed boy named Holbrook.[ii] When Holbrook was airlifted as a 3-year-old the ER nurse at Boston Children's Hospital calmed me down by talking about his eyes, their endless lightness, a possibility of heaven.[iii]

Nantucket skies are a particular blue that occurs when the sun reflects off the sand and water. Artists flock here like right whales in summer to paint under this sky.[iv] There is a crispness in the air—being 30 miles out to sea has its perks. The smog and exhaust fumes from the mainland don't travel this far. The sky fluctuates between a blue so light that it melts into clouds and a blue as intense as a gas flame. At night the blue is a dark indigo funeral robe and on a clear night you can see the Milky Way. One year Mark woke me up at 1 a.m., cajoled with *you'll be sorry if you miss this* as I pleaded *there'll be pictures on the internet*. Despite my objections, we headed to Surfside Beach to see the Leonids meteor shower. Fireballs flitted across the new moon sky to crashing waves.

When I found Mark on the kitchen floor, I could hear the blue jays in the backyard.[v] They hide in the trees and bushes, only showing themselves to chase our cat April until she retreats under the porch. I counted each chest compression to a chorus of blue jays. [vi]

i. Glaciers hold very few air bubbles. The weight of the ice squeezes them out, leaving only the minerals to reflect the blue color. Glacier ice can look brown if it has picked up debris: rocks and shells, fossils and memories. But pure glacial ice? Blue.

ii. Blue eyes hold the least amount of melanin of all the eye colors. More melanin in the front layers of the iris, the darker the color. The lightest blue eyes have barely a drop.

iv. Picasso and Chagall both had blue phases, painting canvasses with variations on the same color, from wet denim saturated blues to featherlight wisps. They were obsessed with this color God chose to limit - blue is the rarest color in nature. There is no naturally occurring compound to color things blue.

v. When we see an azure butterfly, a blue jay, a clear blue sky, or the blue water inside a glacier, we are seeing a trick of light. Blue is not really there.

vi. Mark's lips were the muted blue of stonewashed jeans and faded flannel, barely parted as if trying to keep his last breath in.

**Marigold**

Dear Mark, I left that Monday, goodbye
finger wave as I rushed
to the ferry, knowing you
would feed the dog and cat, make sure
the windows were closed if it rained, keep
our home safe while I was gone.

Six days later stepping
into the kitchen, I was caught
off guard by the dirty
dishes in the sink, the open
refrigerator door, your body
on the floor,
an almost fetal
position, your arm across
your brow, shielding your eyes.

This death is so unlike you—

it shouldn't have been you.
I am the one
who has courted
death, written love
letters to the darkness,
was ready to leave
our two sons motherless
three times. But now I'm not willing
to make them orphans.

Today I flushed the tiny white Percocet pills—
the ones I had hidden
in the medicine cabinet, the exact
number it would take to make my journey
complete, with two added for good measure.

I'm painting most of the walls of our home marigold.

I'm leaving the kitchen alone.

**Keeping Watch**

1. Our cat April thinks she is an unlicensed grief counselor. She lies on her back on the kitchen floor, legs akimbo, arms together on the tile as if in prayer, head turned to her left, eyes closed. Just like I found you. In the exact spot I found you.

2. My first therapist told me to metabolize my grief.

3. Metabolism is the process of converting food to energy, intake to outake. It is what makes it possible for our lungs to take in air, our kidneys to flush the toxins, our legs to run.

4. I can't convert my grief. It is a peachless pit that won't break down.

5. Ancient Egyptians worshiped cats, especially Bastet, the daughter of the gods Ra and Isis. In statues found in tombs she is depicted as a domestic cat, jewels adorning her neck, her nose slightly raised in the air. She was known as a mother who comforted her kittens, a caretaker of the home and family, a protector to souls in the afterlife.

6. Cleo was our first cat—kohl black and named after Cleopatra. She gave birth under our first home on Lang Court to a brood of feral kittens.

7. I tried to tame them, spent hours on the back stoop with food a good six feet away, waiting still and silent for them to eat. The kittens were resolute, and when one bit you, we had to call Animal Control to take them away.

8. We saved Cleo, though, and gave her a name and a home. For months she would sit under the house, call out in a keening wail, wait for her babies to return. I still feel guilty about that.

9. When we first brought Cooper home, his godmother admonished us to keep our cat Cleo out of his bedroom, worried that she would crawl into his crib, snuggle up to his baby warmth, suck the breath from his small mouth, make it her own.

10. It didn't happen.

11. Mark, do you remember that fall day so many years later, the gray breeze whispering against our necks, the sun barely clinging to warmth? Cleo was rubbing up against my leg, insistent for attention, unlike her. I patted her, felt the bones beneath her thin coat, remarked *I don't think she'll make it through another winter.* You reached over and tussled her ear.

12. That evening, when she didn't show up for dinner, you found her behind the shed, curled into herself, her body cooling as the sun slipped away. *I'll take care of her* you told me, and I watched you gently pick her up, hold her body close to your chest, and place her in the hole you dug.

13. Six months later April became a member of the family.

14. When I found you on the kitchen floor, April was there next to you, legs tucked under her body, keeping watch.

# Act III

**Knowing**

Dear Mark, Pi paces from the living room to the library, a circuitous
route that doesn't change, the clicking of his too long nails announcing
his arrival.

He is nervous,

this dog you never wanted but agreed to adopt because of me.
I can be persuasive when the mood suits me.

This dog became a part of our family, softly jumping to hug you
when you walked in the door, holding back just enough of his strength

so he didn't knock you down. The look of consternation in his brown eyes
as he whined to cover your face with licking kisses hello.

I remember catching you both watching the Red Sox together,
his head on your lap as you stroked his court jester ears.

You loved him.

And as he sat with you as you took your last breath, you both silent
on the tile floor of the kitchen, I'm sure he knew in the same way

the morning glories you planted in the front yard know that closing
is inevitable.

**Deluge**

Dear Mark,
remember
when you came by
after softball
sweaty
hungry
i wasn't prepared
to feed you
caught off guard
after only
one date
so we walked
to China City
one block east
two blocks north
not expecting
the rain
as we waited
at the take-out
window a Florida
deluge
warm
tropical
making rivers in
the road, flooding
the sidewalk
our shoes
we huddled
under the awning
decided to
risk it
run back
with our food
jumping
over puddles
laughing
when we missed
until we reached
my porch

we ate
on the patio
the rain
clouds
rushing
west
giving way
to a sky
so blue
it hurt

**I ate the mango**

you brought home
last week from Stop
& Shop, still green

as you prematurely
anticipated peak season.

I don't like mangoes.

I don't like the sound
of the knife as it cuts
through the flesh, hits

the hard pulpy pit. Or how
the juice slides down my fingers,
makes them itch. But the mango

was ripe, red burnished by the sun
that finds its way into our kitchen
window, only one swath of yellow remained.

I didn't want it to go to waste.

# Life

Against last night's new snow—
a jagged drop of blood, pinpoint
of crimson surrounded by concentric
circles of ombre pinks, craggy pines and
barren birches standing guard, the sky

a mourning dove gray. My dog, Pi, runs
to investigate, begins licking the tinted ground.

We see it is one of many—a breadcrumb
path leading back into the trees
on the other side. Pi runs ahead,
his shepherd bark sounding an
alarm, driven by sight instead of
smell, while I struggle to keep up,

trudging through the unmarked
whiteness. The drops become larger, deeper
red, until we find her, her winter fur
brown and heavy, embellished with a smattering
of snow crystals catching the filtered sunlight.

Hunting season is over but we can see the hole
left by the rifle, an oval rink of blood surrounding her.

I kneel next to her, gaze into her hickory
eyes, wonder if she has a fawn that is
missing her, a sister doe sniffing the air
for her scent. The sky fills with crows as Pi
barks commands, expecting
her to rise up, confused that she isn't
running away.

## There are days I think you are a bird

maybe the cardinal
that sits
on the window-
sill by my desk
while I write.
Or the red-
bellied woodpecker
that clears
his throat
between bouts
of bug searching
while I wait
on the deck,
morning coffee
in hand. I could
believe
you are the squirrel
with the tail
so bushy
it should
topple over,
but doesn't,
the one
that frequents
the maple tree, staying
just far up enough
to aggravate
Pi, make him stand
at attention, waiting
for a chase. Deer
use the front yard
as a highway
but you couldn't
be one of them,
so skittish
they run
from the motion
sensor light.
I am sure you are

the hummingbird
that levitates
in front of
the dining room
window, so
still as if held
by the hand
of God.

**Break**

Bone weary after a day of packing
pots and pans, bedding, the dulcimer
you gave me on our last anniversary,
I go outside under the new moon sky,
soft breeze filters through the scrub
oak, pines, the cotton of my last
unpacked clean shirt. Above the spot
where the Boston Whaler sat missing
the sluice of summer waters, now
in some other boater's yard, a shooting star
surprises the endless night, adagio on a velvet
backdrop, staccato of memories
following. I watch long after the darkness
returns, resting, waiting, hoping for another

**Hummingbird Season**

I missed hummingbird
season, the Mexican mi-
gration coming home.

March became Novem-
ber before I found my foot-
ing. Your death, cold sand.

I dream of iridescent
green feathers, wings beat-
ing so fast they appear to
stop time, levitate
above footprints in the mud.

A year goes quickly
counting days by the stirrings
of translucent wings.

I'll take the feeder
down tomorrow—plan better
for next year—alone.

## A Year of Firsts

First Memorial Day on thick Crane stationary writing thank-you notes instead of cooking hot dogs for you and veggie burgers for me on the grill. *Thank you for the flowers. Thank you for the casserole.*

First Flag Day searching for the flagpole you bought for the front of the house, and not finding it.

First July 4 without the Main Street water fight, watermelon eating contest, cook-out at Miacomet Beach, or fireworks off Jetties Beach.

First birthday without a card from you.

First Halloween without you wearing the Dracula mask you wear every year, with the rainbow colored clown hair, carrying an empty bag just in case there's extra candy. (This year we didn't go trick-or-treating.)

First Thanksgiving without a television—I gave it away—so first Thanksgiving without football, the spot on the couch empty except for Pi, our dog. It is now his favorite place.

First December packing up—a brown vista of small U-Haul boxes, and medium, and large, including wardrobe boxes for hanging clothes, and cylindrical boxes for lamps, rectangle boxes for dishes with special padded envelopes, and small sturdy boxes for books. Lots of books. But I did give a few away—you would have been proud.

First Christmas playing Santa alone. First Christmas without leaving out cookies and milk. First Christmas where none of us rushed into the living room before dawn. (We all slept past 10 a.m.)

First New Year's Eve where I went to sleep early. On purpose. And not because I began drinking bourbon too early.

First New Year's Day spent unpacking - looking for the coffeemaker (we left it behind), the hammer (it's with the coffeemaker), the dog bed (how could we forget that?), the vacuum.

First morning in a new bed, in a new home, on a new street, in a new town. First home without memories of you walking through the front door.

**Counting Minutes**

Dropping seconds like oak leaves in late fall,
the clocks in this house keep misplacing time,
as if air here is heavier and time
must     trudge    between.

Every day they are one minute slower.
I reset them all each morning. It has
become a dream-like walk through my morning,
a ritual that happens pre-coffee.

I understand the old wall clock I brought
from the home we shared. But I can't make sense
of my new watch, the bedside clock
or the languishing song of the cuckoo.

I'm giving up this constant resetting.
I'm choosing to live inside this new time.

**Wildfire**

His anger is a lightning storm in the
iris of his eyes, our son who masks his
grief with side glances and nods. I worry
about him, knowing how easy it is
for sparks to become wildfires. Scared
to feel the burning of my soles, I hesitate
before stepping on hot coals, unable
to turn away. There is a part of me that is jealous,
so jealous of this fire that is alive
as it threatens to consume, hides
in the hollowed-out holes left by
your death, leaves silence in its path.
And now the collapsing embers are glowing.
He is tinder. And the fire is hungry.

**Ice Storm**

Dear Mark, the weather report calls for ice
storms. I don't know what to do. I fear
the pipes will freeze and burst. No one wrapped them
with insulation as you did in our
home. And ice melt. I bought what was on sale,
forgetting what you used.

I've unpacked the quilts and blankets that made
the move in case the power goes out. The
rain turns to sleet, I gather up flashlights,
candles, matches, water. I lost your
propane camping lanterns. I'm sorry.
Ice shrouds birch branches outside my bedroom
window. It catches the sun, makes broken
prisms, colors the wall.

## When Spring is a Lie You Tell Yourself

The magnolia tree burst alive
from bare branches to flowers last week—
early, I thought, since it's barely
March. But what do I know?
I have the opposite of a green
thumb. Plants in the garden
section shrink when I walk by,
hoping I won't pick them
for early death in my yard.
I watched the gray pussy willows
birth into pink-tinged petals, so delicate
they resemble a newborn's lips
upturned in its first smile. Then yesterday
snowflakes swept across the yard. A mid-March
freeze. I watched as the delicate flowers
drooped on the gray branches, tears
of pink flowers giving up, letting go.
Today I'll rake up the brown shrivels
that have fallen to the ground, deadhead
those refusing to give up.

**Temporary Permanence**

There is a bird's nest outside my bedroom window
                         of the new home we've made without him.

I watch each day hoping to see a cardinal
                                   chickadee
                                          or robin
                          snuggled in between the braided twigs.

I know that nests are a temporary shelter, a way station
         for some on their journey through, a spec home for others
                 who stick around but keep building, never using
         the same nest twice. I shouldn't keep watching and expecting

but I do.

A part of me wants to believe a pair of goldfinches will
         return, replenish the missing moss, fluff up the bed, settle in.

Spring is coming.                                So I keep watching.

## Hope

*Hope is the thing with feathers*
*—Emily Dickinson*

If hope is a feathered thing, we're
doomed. My cat has been known to decimate
cardinals in the bathtub, serve up mewling
baby rabbits, spastic noses searching
for their mama's milky scent, droplets
of blood staining the floor.

Meadow mice were easy prey, abundant
in the woods by our home. In spring
she would deliver two or three a week
sometimes still alive, more often half-eaten.

The snake was the worst—
captured by her on a leaden crystal
fall day, too cold for it to escape
until she carried it into the kitchen,
warm from baking bread.

He slithered behind the
oven as she stared, waiting
for him to re-emerge, eventually
giving up and sauntering away.

We found his dried body the next spring.

**Redemption**

We heard him hit the window
before we saw him, this spring
robin enjoying the rare Ohio
sunny day, now supine on the
ground, twig legs reaching
for the blue sky. I rushed outside.
Anxious to see if he was still
alive, I gently picked him up.
My thumb stroked the satin
feathers on his back, his heartbeat
slowing in my palm.

To be honest, I cried.

Not sobbing as has been my usual
these days. But slow tears working
their way down my raw cheeks.
I held him for minutes that felt
much longer, before

he finally opened
his eyes, moved his head
to look at me fully.
I didn't want
to let him go.

I placed him on the front step, sat
next to him to keep him safe. He took
flight, flapped his uninjured wings as small
chest feathers snowed down and new buds
from the dogwood bounced under his weight.

## Acknowledgments

The following poems have been previously published or in the form seen here or slightly altered:

"We are birthed in music" in the June 2023 summer issues of *Thimble Lit Magazine.*

"The Act of Dying" (page 15) in the October 2023 fall edition of *Still: The Journal.*

"Quilting" in the October 2023 fall edition of *Still: The Journal.*

"I put your boots on today" in the 2019 anthology *Women Speak: Women of Appalachia Project.*

"New Moon" in the June 2022 issue of *Sheila-Na-Gig* online literary magazine.

"There are days I think you are a bird" in the July 2023 edition of *The Wise Owl.*

**Lucretia Voigt** is a fifth-generation Appalachian who inherited her love of the musical cadence of words from her ancestors. Growing up in Eastern Kentucky, she turned to poetry to make sense of her world, to ask questions when life seemed confusing, and to provide solace during dark times. The Act of Dying was born from her desire to be truly present in the journey she found herself walking as she experienced the deaths of her brother in 2007 and her husband in 2021. Unexpected deaths are like being thrown from a helicopter into an icy lake, coming up for air and realizing the shore is miles away. Poetry became a raft in that lake, a stopping point where she could rest, catch her breath, gather her strength to continue. She found that grief is both painful and beautiful, agony and joy, paralyzing and freeing.

www.ingramcontent.com/pod-product-compliance
Lightning Source LLC
Chambersburg PA
CBHW030059170426
43197CB00010B/1585